FORTUNE-T[illegible]
TEA LEAVES

An up-to-date guide to reading the future in the bottom of your tea cup.

By the same author

THE FORTUNE-TELLER'S WORKBOOK
FORTUNE-TELLING BY TAROT CARDS
THE LIVING HAND (with Malcolm Wright)
MOON SIGNS
RISING SIGNS
TAROT IN ACTION!

FORTUNE-TELLING BY TEA LEAVES

A PRACTICAL GUIDE TO THE ANCIENT ART OF TASSEOGRAPHY

Sasha Fenton

THE AQUARIAN PRESS

First published 1987

British Library Cataloguing in Publication Data

Fenton, Sasha
Fortune-telling by tea leaves : a practical guide to the ancient art of tasseography.
1. Fortune-telling by tea leaves
I. Title
133.3'244 BF1881

ISBN 0-85030-657-4

The Aquarian Press is part of the Thorsons Publishing Group, Wellingborough, Northamptonshire, NN8 2RQ, England

Printed in Great Britain by Richard Clay Limited, Bungay, Suffolk

3 5 7 9 10 8 6 4

CONTENTS

Acknowledgements 7
Introduction 9

Chapter
1. A Memorable Reading 13
2. How to Make Tea 16
3. Preparation 18
4. Symbols Associated With Other Divinations 25
5. A Dictionary of Tea Leaf Symbols 30
6. Examples of Readings 104

'Love and scandal are the best sweeteners of tea'

Henry Fielding (22/4/1707 – 8/10/1754)
from *Love in Several Masques*, IV.xi

ACKNOWLEDGEMENTS

Many thanks to Tony Fenton for putting up with 'real tea' for a month when he much prefers cheap and cheerful tea bags. Also to Linda Tulley for word processing and much tea drinking in the name of research. Thanks to Denise Russell for passing on her knowledge of the subject, and also to Jason Russell for some of the illustrations. Thanks to Nina Ashby for helping with research and for free use of her collection of unusual books and esoteric information.

INTRODUCTION

Tea-leaf reading as a method of divination can be categorized as intuitive art with an infusion of definitive psychic skill. There is a background of well-known symbolic shapes which can be learned by heart (for instance, a tea-leaf in the shape of a dog would indicate a good friend). However, the greatest aid is to have the kind of imagination which can be encouraged to grow into true psychic ability.

Tea-leaf reading, or tasseography, works in the same way as sand reading, or geomancy; it is both the area of the cup (or sand tray) plus the shapes which are formed, plus the use of a free flowing imagination, which leads to the development of those psychic powers which make the whole thing work. In countries where tea is not habitually drunk, coffee grounds are used in much the same way, but I think Readers would use a number of grounds grouped together rather than looking at each group individually. As far as tea is concerned, a single leaf can be read, two or three grouped together may make a picture, or a whole lot may group themselves together into a discernible shape. It doesn't matter how they arrange themselves or what you make of them; if your imagination if flowing freely you can't go wrong.

Familiarly-shaped objects such as dogs, flowers, birds, etc. have much the same kind of meanings as they do in the interpretation of dreams because most of these objects do crop up again and again in many forms of divination. One could, with a certain amount of adaptation, use the shape meanings which are listed in this book as a reference for unravelling dreams, for reading the shapes which form in the flickering flames of a fire, or for reading clouds, sand, coffee, flights of birds or a myriad of other things. There is nothing new in all this except for the more modern kind of shape such as an aeroplane.

Astrological symbolism can be used, as can the Tarot, playing cards, maybe even the Kabbalah. Some of these ideas are ancient and well-known, but I have made a few suggestions of my own based upon my experience.

The Aura

I was discussing this project with a very psychic friend of mine who suggested that the Enquirer's aura could possibly be attached to the cup for a while after drinking, and this made a lot of sense to me. I know many psychics, myself included, who could never bring themselves to buy second-hand clothes, whatever kind of a bargain they appeared to be. This is because they have been worn within the aura of someone unknown who might have left goodness-knows-what-traces behind. For exactly the same reason, psychics will buy a second-hand object simply because it *feels* right and still carries an aura of peace or love within it. This aura may be something intrinsic to the object or something which has become attached to it from its previous owner. People who feel that a particular house has 'good vibrations' are using the same kind of notion. A tea cup, of course, is washed up after use and it would not necessarily be used by the same person each time, however the aura of the last person to drink from it would remain attached for a while at least. This action would be intensified if the Enquirer knew that his cup was due to be read after he had finished his drink, because this would focus his mind and add power to the thought and feelings embedded in his aura.

Advice and Warnings

I'm afraid that I have to repeat the same rather boring warning which all professional Readers give about all forms of divination: *do not frighten your Enquirer*. Even if you are only working with a couple of friends for a giggle, watch what you say. Even those who seem to be scoffing will take what you say *very seriously* and frequently remember what was said to them for years afterwards.

If you really feel that you are looking at something bad, then do tone it down. Tell your Enquirers by all means, but in a gentle and positive way. For instance, if you thought you could detect a forthcoming illness in the cup, tell them that they must take things a bit easier and not neglect any potential health problem as they seemed to be over-stressed or overdoing things. If time proves that you are right, then at least *you* have had confirmation of your ability.

As a professional Reader, I am often asked what I do when I see something bad during a reading. The answer is that this depends upon a good many circumstances. For instance, if the reading is a 'quicky' which is being given in a bookshop as a part of a publicity promotion, I would probably keep any difficult thoughts to myself. This is chiefly because I haven't the time under those circumstances to double check by other means of divination whether I am right, and it would be totally wrong of me to give off-the-cuff predictions of disaster if I weren't even sure that I was right! In those circumstances I wouldn't have time to give the correct kind of counselling which has to accompany the giving of bad news. Of course, when clients come to my home for a private reading, I pass on everything I see. This is because firstly, they have paid good money for a reading and therefore are entitled to hear what there is to hear, and secondly, I would have the time to check my findings. Finally, under such controlled circumstances, I would have the time to counsel clients and allow them to come to terms with their potential situation and to talk it over in peace and quiet.

Even then, if I thought a client was utterly neurotic and completely incapable of handling *any* kind of problem, I would hold back except for handing out the kind of gentle advice which I outlined earlier. This may be a 'cop out' in terms of avoiding trouble for myself, but I consider that it is one to which I am entitled. There is a limit to what a Reader has to do for a client. If the client really needs a psychiatrist, and a good many clients do, then that is what they must find; it is not up to Readers, however skilled and however caring, to live other people's life for them – although there are plenty of clients who would be happy for us to do just that.

History and Background

Tea was first grown and drunk in China. Tea cultivation then spread round the Orient with different kinds of tea being grown in different places. The taste of the tea depends both upon the kind of bush which is planted and the type of soil and environment it grows in. China tea is larger leafed, more fragrant and weaker than Indian tea; it is drunk without the addition of milk, sugar or lemon. As it happens, the Chinese and Japanese loathe milk or dairy foods even today, and in times gone by these products were never used for human consumption until the 'foreign devils' came to the East. Tea-leaf divination definitely started in China and travelled south and east with both the spread of tea drinking and with the migrations of the Gypsies. Romanies spring originally from these areas of Northern India, West Pakistan and Afghanistan, which were the centre of the Mogul Empire, therefore they would have developed both the tea drinking habit and the ability to read the future in the leaves. Perhaps Americans read coffee grounds. I know that some nations do and it works in much the same way as tea-leaf reading.

Psychic development

There is an upsurge of interest in psychic and spiritual matters today. People of all types want to understand just that little bit more of life from a deeper point of view. Teacup reading is an excellent way of training the mind to be receptive to psychic vibrations. It has rather gone out of fashion these days – Tarot is far more popular – but this is a shame because the rate of development would be even faster using this kind of method as it unlocks one's imagination. Whenever you do any psychic work it is advisable to take a couple of precautions. Firstly, before doing anything, ask the spirits to help you give your Enquirer worthwhile advice. When you have completely finished, imagine yourself climbing into a sleeping bag and closing it up completely over your head. This will 'close you down' and prevent any unwanted psychic disturbances bothering you. This idea was given to me by a professional psychic called David Bingham.

1

A MEMORABLE READING

I remember as clearly as if it were only last week spending a wet and dreary afternoon in our neighbour's house. I was about seven years of age. These kind neighbours looked after me some afternoons after school until my mother returned from work. They had a daughter called Jeanette who was around my own age.

On this particular afternoon, Jeanette and I were thoroughly bored and didn't seem to summon up any interest in our usual games and pastimes. Mrs Laudrum noticed that neither of us had completely finished our cups of tea. We complained that the tea had too many leaves in it and told her that she would have to buy herself a new tea-strainer as the leaves were falling through the hole in the battered old one. She looked at the dregs of leafy tea which remained in our cups and asked if we would like her to tell us our fortunes. We were instantly galvanized and transformed from being two bored and listless kids to being fully alert, our eyes and ears popping with interest.

Mrs Laudrum told us to hold our cups and swirl the tea around in them three times. After that she took Jeanette's cup and placed it upside down on her saucer. She turned the cup three times in the saucer and then proceeded to tell Jeanette's fortune. I don't remember a word she told her but I do remember being riveted by the ceremony of it all and feeling shivery with the anticipation of something magical again about to happen.

She then took my cup and went through the same procedure. She sat and concentrated for quite a while, much longer than she had for Jeanette. Her hands went up to her face and she started to rub at a patch in the centre of her forehead. The tension mounted: I *knew* something out of the ordinary was happening. Mrs Laudrum began to speak.

'You are in for a lot of trouble over the next few years,' she said. 'There are going to be some problems concerning your family and this will affect your life badly for a while, but you mustn't become too down-hearted because you will have a lot to look forward to.' At this point she seemed to go off into a bit of a dream and didn't speak again for a few minutes. I still sat spellbound and so did Jeanette.

Mrs Laudrum then seemed to get her second wind. 'You will travel a lot, by every kind of transport. I can see boats, trains, motor-cars and even aeroplanes.' It was unheard of at that time for ordinary people to travel in aeroplanes. She went on: 'After a few early problems you will become quite renowned and could even become rich as a result of some kind of special work.' I butted in, 'Dancing, I expect.' I was training even at that young age for a stage career.

'No, not dancing. Not dancing,' she repeated, 'writing, I think, also travelling around to speak to people about something special. You will have a strange life, you will meet many people, some of them will be famous and important, but you could experience more heartache than most people do. You will never lack courage, but sometimes people who you thought were your friends will let you down. Jealous probably. A strange life,' she repeated, 'riches, fame, something very unusual, and sorrows too, but always travelling and always able to pick yourself up and start again, although the need for this will be less and less as you pass into middle age. You will never want for money, especially as you get older.'

Well, obviously something happened during this reading. I asked Mrs Laudrum how she did it and she showed me how the leaves formed themselves into the shapes of birds and animals and so on and how these birds and things represented travel, tears, etc. To be honest, I think Mrs Laudrum would be the first to say that this wasn't strictly speaking a *tea-leaf reading* but a futuristic clairvoyant reading of a superb standard. In all the subsequent years of my association with the Laudrum family, I never saw her read the leaves again, for me or for anyone else. If that one event had never occurred, I would never have known she could even do such a thing and would never have had my eyes opened to the world of divination.

Within five years of this reading, I was teaching myself to read hands and playing cards. I didn't return to the tea-leaves for many years, by which time I knew that my own clairvoyant powers were pretty well advanced. But even now, as a fully-fledged professional, I would be more than proud to be able to produce a reading like the one she did that day.

Incidentally, I *did* have a great many problems due to the fact that both my father and my uncle died leaving my aunt and mother to raise three children and look after two elderly parents between them. My aunt was always rather frail so mother had to bring in most of the money; all this meant I was left alone a lot. I filled in any spare time after being at school and at nearby dancing schools by reading and drawing, also by writing. My imagination had a great deal of time in which to develop, which has, of course, been a great help in my subsequent career as a Reader.

Bless you Jane Laudrum wherever you are.

2

HOW TO MAKE TEA

It may seem totally ridiculous to tell people how to make tea, but nowadays we have a whole generation of tea-bag stirrers growing up who have no idea of how properly-brewed tea should be prepared!

1 Empty the kettle and refill it with freshly drawn cold water. Whilst this is heating up, assemble the teapot, tea, crockery, milk, etc.
2 Just before the water comes to the boil, pour a little of it into the teapot, swill it around the pot and pour it away. This has the dual purpose of removing any dust from the pot and also warming it.
3 Place one rounded (not heaped) teaspoon of tea per person in the pot. The old books used to say 'one per person plus one for the pot' but unless you are using a good quality large-leaf tea such as Earl Grey or Darjeeling, this makes the brew terribly strong.
4 When you wish to pour the boiling water over the tea leaves, take the pot to the kettle, not the kettle to the pot.
5 Pour the water over the tea leaves as soon as it comes to the boil. Overboiling takes the oxygen out of the water and makes it taste hard and metallic.
6 Put the lid on the teapot and leave the tea to brew for a few minutes. The old books used to say leave it for five minutes but this produces a *stewed* flavour which is unpalatable to modern day tastes.

When I was a child, I can remember arguments raging as to whether the milk or the tea should be put into the cup first. If the milk is put in first, the tea will mix together with the milk instantly; if it is added after, it will need stirring. The latter is actually correct and it is for this reason that a teaspoon should always be provided, whether the tea drinkers take sugar or not. Of course, as far as divination is concerned, it doesn't matter whether one drinks tea with or without milk. One should not, of course, use a strainer, as the object is to allow a few of the tea leaves to fall into the cup. It is also a good idea to use a shallower type of cup with no pattern on the inside. A mug is no good as it is too deep and the bottom has a rigid 'corner', whereas a cup slopes more shallowly.

3

PREPARATION

Use a teacup rather than a mug. The rather shallow type of cup with a plain interior is the best; patterns and fluting will interfere with the reading. Ask the Enquirer to swirl the tea round in the cup in an *anti-clockwise* direction three times using his or her left hand. Then ask them to place the cup upside down onto the saucer. Either you or the Enquirer should now turn the cup three times in an *anti-clockwise* direction, once again using the left hand.

After this, turn the cup over, keeping the handle towards you, tilt it to a convenient angle and take a good long look inside.

Location of Events (See Fig. 1)

The handle represents the Enquirier, therefore any leaves in that area suggest events concerning him or her or occurring in their home area. The opposite side of the cup refers to strangers and events away from the home.

Symbols which point towards the handle are approaching the Enquirer and symbols which point away from the handle suggest people or situations which are leaving the Enquirer. The bottom of the cup shows sorrows, the top shows joys.

Timing of Events (See Fig. 2)

The rim of the cup is the near future, half way down shows events within a few months, while the area close to the bottom shows the distant future. If there are any numbers visible, these can help with the timing of events. For instance, an anchor (which would signify a journey)

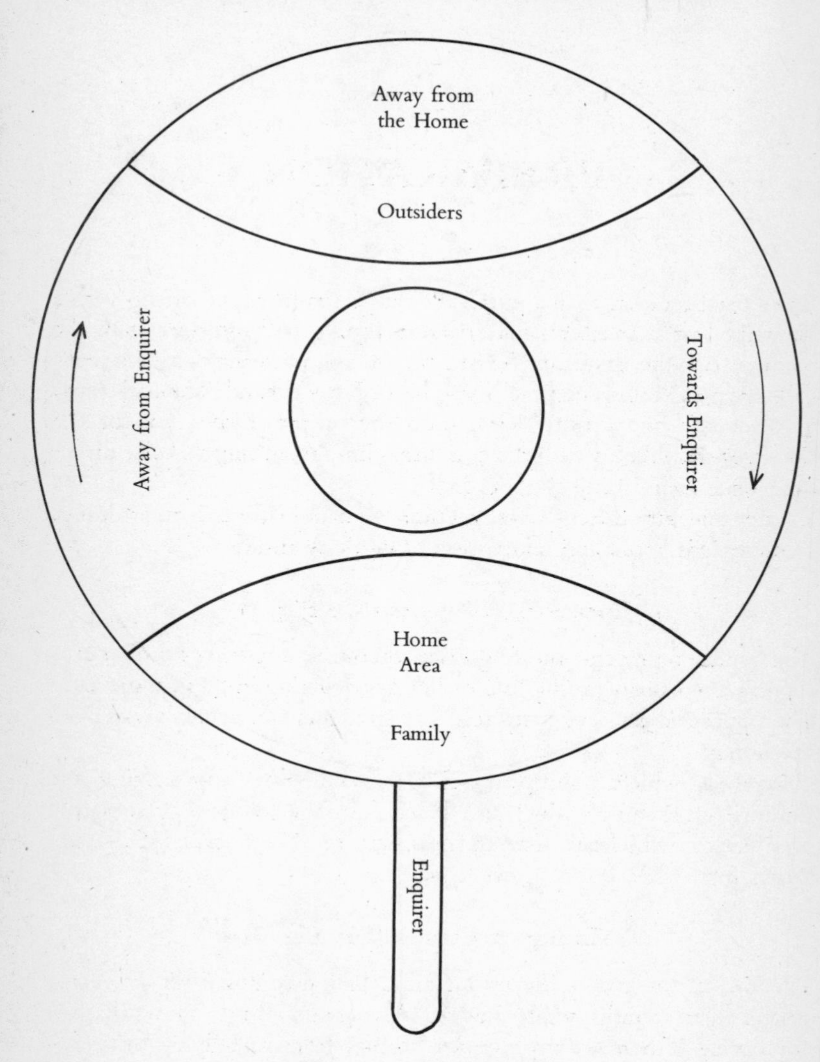

Figure 1 Location of Events

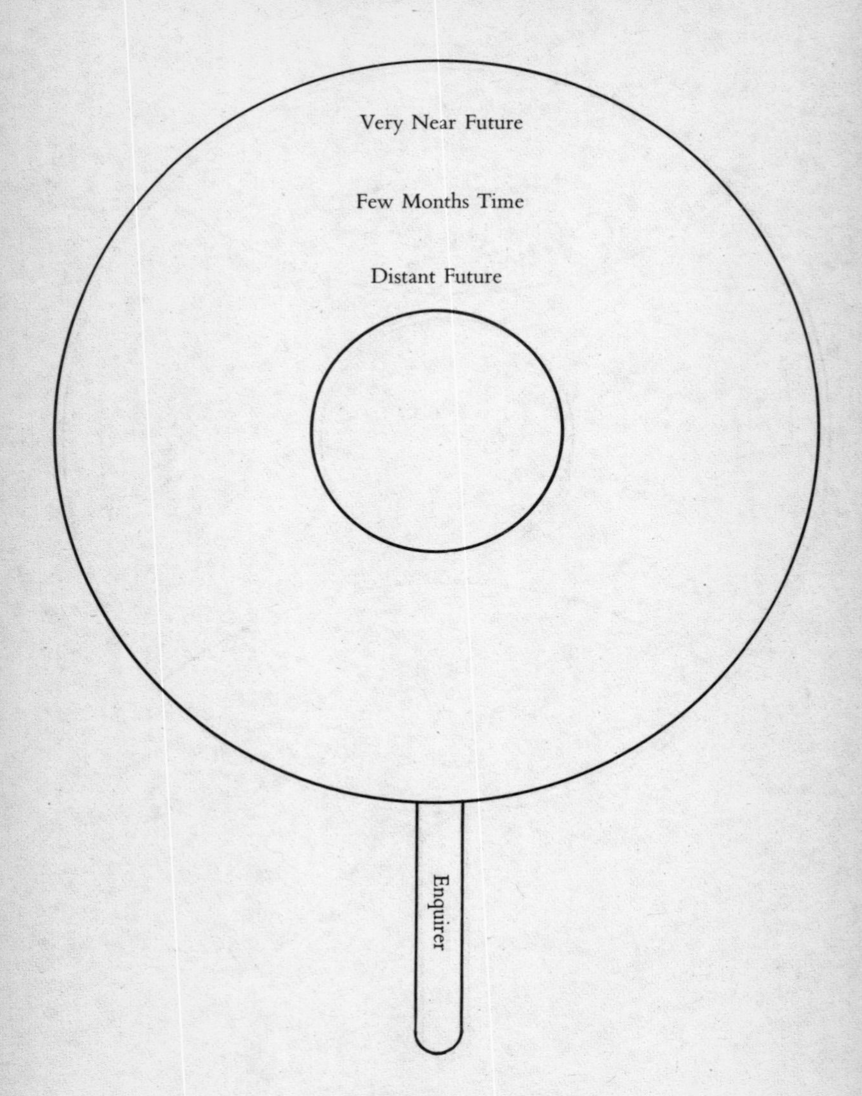

Figure 2 Timing of Events

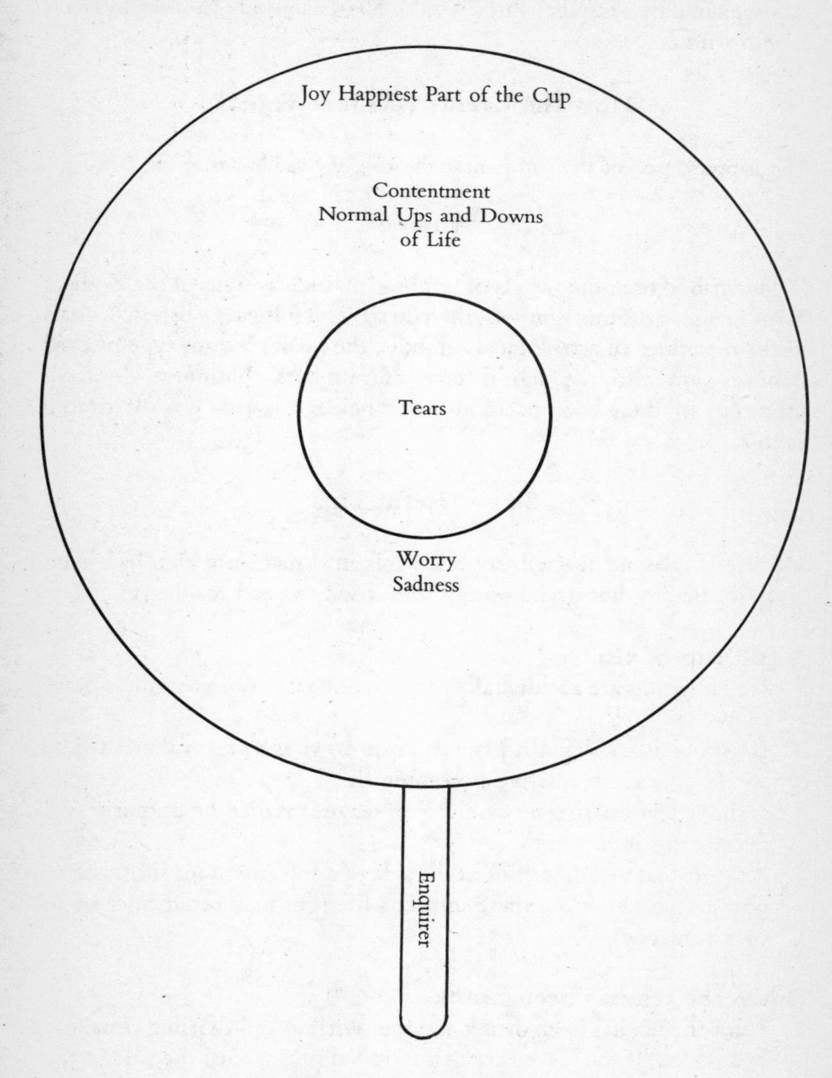

Figure 3 How the Events Feel

accompanied by a number three would tell of a journey to come in three month's time.

How the Events Feel (See Fig. 3)

The happiest part of the cup is near the rim, the saddest is at the bottom.

Symbols

If you wish to use other kinds of symbolism, such as signs of the Zodiac, Tarot images or Runic symbols, then do so. The following lists give clues to the meanings of astrological symbols, the most obvious type of card symbols and also the significance of numbers. Numbers do have meanings of their own in addition to being a useful way of timing events.

Some Useful Tips

My friend, Denise Russell, supplied this information which had been given to her by her grandmother who used to read tea-leaves.

A full cup of tea

1 If two spoons are accidentally put into one saucer, there will be news of twins.
2 If a spoon is accidentally placed upside down in a saucer there will be news of a close relative becoming ill.
3 A single leaf floating on a full cup of tea means that the Enquirer will be coming into money.
4 A single leaf which is stuck at the side of a full cup of tea shows news of a stranger entering the Enquirer's life (this may be advance news of a romance).

When the tea has been drunk

1 After the tea has been drunk and the swirling and twirling ritual has been done, if the leaves are in a rounded pile against the side of the cup which is on the opposite side to the handle, there is trouble com-

ing. This trouble is *not* of the Enquirer's own doing and it will come without warning.

2 If the leaves are rounded up on the handle side, there will also be trouble, but this time it will be of the Enquirer's own doing.

Denise mentioned that her grandmother always told her that only intuitive people *asked* for a reading and when they did so, they would hear good news and good of themselves, whereas if a Reader felt impelled to offer a reading to someone, there would always be bad or sad news. I have found this holds true for other kinds of readings as well. If I feel *compelled* to give someone a reading, there is always some kind of warning to come out of the reading.

Further tea-leaf lore

My mother-in-law used to say that if two people poured out of the same pot, one of them would have a baby on the way by the end of the year. The old joke was that the 'baby' would turn out to be ginger twins!

Letters of the alphabet signify the names of people who will be important to the Enquirer in the future. A symbol which is found close to the letter will give a clue as to how the person will affect the Enquirer. For instance, the letter 'A' accompanied by a monkey might indicate a gossipy person whose name begins with 'A' whom the Enquirer must be wary of. The position of the letter and accompanying symbol will give a clue as to where this person might be found. For instance, if near the handle, it will happen around the Enquirer's home; if away from the handle, away from the home.

Stalks represent people, often strangers. A long firm stalk represents a man while a shorter thinner one suggests a woman. If a straight stalk is found, the stranger will be reliable, while a bendy one indicates a fickle friend or someone who is not in a position to help the Enquirer much. Slanted stalks show unreliable or untrustworthy people. The colour of the stalk could give a clue to the colouring of the person.

If your Enquirer wants to know when he or she is likely to get married, you can try this ruse. Take a clean dry teaspoon and balance it on the edge of the cup. Pour a little tea into the bowl of the spoon a drop at a time until the spoon falls into the cup; the number of drops shows the number of years the Enquirer will have to wait. Rings show marriage. If a ring is near the rim the marriage will be happy; it also shows that marriage is probably not far off for the Enquirer. Broken rings or rings at the bottom of the cup show broken marriages or unhappiness in marriage. A double ring could indicate two marriages or one which the Enquirer rushes into and then regrets later. A bell is also a sign of a wedding.

Lucky signs are horseshoes, circles and rings, flowers, trees, animals and crowns; also the number seven. Triangles are usually lucky but if they are found at the bottom of the cup or with the apex pointing downwards, there could be a spell of bad luck ahead or something which has been all right so far but which could begin to become difficult. A triangle which points upwards denotes a win or a legacy to come. Another interpretation is a fortunate meeting connected with money.

Squares represent protection and restriction. If a dangerous symbol (such as an arrow) appears facing towards the handle (therefore towards the Enquirer), this shows that a letter containing bad news will be on the way, but if there is a square around the arrow, the Enquirer will be protected from the worst. A square can show a restricting situation for the Enquirer such as a commitment to an unsatisfactory job. Squares seem to show safety even if that protection is rather restrictive. Crosses of all kinds mean sadness and problems to be faced.

Dots always symbolize money. If the dots are close to another symbol, read them together. Mountains show efforts which will have to be made while clouds show illusion and muddled problems. Lines represent journeys; clear straight lines show good journeys while broken or wavering ones suggest problems en route.

4

SYMBOLS ASSOCIATED WITH OTHER DIVINATIONS

Astrological Symbols

Aries ♈
Start of an enterprise. Self-motivation, courage and optimism. Blind faith and foolishness.

Taurus ♉
Sorting out priorities and personal values. Money, possessions and ownership. Beauty, culture, art and music. Matters relating to building, property and land.

Gemini ♊
Neighbours and local matters. Forms of local travel and transport. Communications and documents. Business, especially sales. Sport and education. Brothers and sisters.

Cancer ♋
Home, security and family. Mother figures. One's own business, especially shops. Emotions and moods. Caring for others, including care for animals.

Leo ♌
Children, romantic lovers. Creative projects, pastimes, hobbies and some sports. Holidays and fun. Pride in achievement – either one's own or one's children's.

Virgo ♍
Work, duties to employers and employees. Health and hospitals. Food and nutrition. Clothing. Selection, choice, discrimination.

Libra ♎
Partnerships and co-operation. Marriage or other steady relationships. Open enemies. Beauty, culture and food. New joint business enterprises.

Scorpio ♏
Commitments, firm relationships. Joint finances. Birth, death, sex and all deeper matters. Psychic and mediumistic matters. Police and medicine.

Sagittarius ♐
The law. Philosophy and religion. Higher education. Travel, freedom and lack of commitment. Matters related to large animals, especially horses.

Capricorn ♑
Public life, status and positions of responsibility. Aims and ambitions. Career and work, especially big business. Struggle and effort which is worthwhile in the long term. Help from those in authority. Father figures.

Aquarius ♒
Friends, detached relationships. Group activities, clubs and societies. Education. Astrology. Computers and other modern technology. Pride, courage but also arrogance.

Pisces ♓
Creativity. Mysticism. Private life, private sorrows. Self-sacrifice. Secret enemies. Dreams and desires, illusion and delusion. Mood changes which come from a shift in one's conciousness. Association with places of confinement.

Tarot symbols

Wands (or Staves)
Enthusiasm, new ventures, new people entering the Enquirer's life. Problems which can be overcome. Travel for pleasure, creativity of an intellectual kind.

Cups
Emotional matters, love, marriage, family life. The past. Creation of beautiful things.

Swords
Troubles, illness, swift action to be taken. Quarrels and separations. Endings which pave the way for a fresh start. Courageous creativity.

Pentacles (or Coins)
Money matters, practicalities, property and land, possessions. Business, finance and the start or completion of large-scale projects. Personal values. Creativity of a practical kind.

Playing card symbols

Clubs ♣
Good luck, especially concerning money. New enterprises which will work out well for the Enquirer. Helpful people around the Enquirer. Education.

Diamonds ♦
Money, a win. Sometimes the gift of a ring, possibly indicating marriage to come. Practicalities, especially where money is concerned.

Hearts ♥
Happiness and abundance. Marriage and homelife. The birth of a child or the beginning of a creative enterprise. Satisfaction and completion.

Spades ♠
Troubles, arguments, losses, bad luck and sadness. This could indicate the end of a relationship. Death of a situation which clears the way for a fresh start. Health problems for the Enquirer or his/her family.

Numbers

One
Similar to the zodiac sign of Leo. A sign of creativity which may foretell the birth of a baby, or the birth of a project of some kind for the Enquirer. Could also mean a holiday or a romance to come.

Two
Like the zodiac sign of Cancer. This may tell of a move of house or work to be done on the Enquirer's present home. There may be news concerning older females in the family. Security will be important.

Three
Similar to the zodiac signs of Aries and Scorpio. This suggests efforts to be made in the near future. The Enquirer will have to take a bold step forwards but should be warned against losing his or her temper or having silly accidents.

Four
Similar to the zodiac signs of Gemini and Virgo. This concerns communications, so the Enquirer could expect important letters soon or some news about neighbourhood matters. Work and services to be done, especially those requiring concentration, will be important, as will health matters.

Five
Like the zodiac sign of Sagittarius. This could mean legal matters to be settled soon. A long journey over water is a possibility, as is anything which will broaden the Enquirer's mind either directly by experience or by education.

Six
Like Taurus and Libra. This suggests that beauty and harmony are going to be important soon. There could be an interesting hobby involving the creation of beautiful things or there could be a romance on the way.

Seven
Like the zodiac sign of Capricorn. This means that serious matters will need to be attended to soon. There could be dealings with people in positions of authority. The Enquirer's work will be important soon, as will his public image and status.

Eight
Similar to the zodiac sign of Aquarius. This shows increasing independence on behalf of the Enquirer plus a certain level of eccentricity to come. He or she could behave in an uncharacteristic manner for a while or could be subject to unexpected events in his or her life soon.

Nine
Like the zodiac sign of Pisces. This could bring the Enquirer romance, inspiration and immense kindness from others but it could also bring muddle, illusion and bad judgement in some important matter.

5

A DICTIONARY OF TEA LEAF SYMBOLS

In the cases where symbols have more than one interpretation, or where slight differences in appearance or position actually *alter* the meaning, all the possible interpretations are given.

Acorn

The start of something which is destined to grow into maturity and success, also a long life and good fortune. If it is in the middle area of the cup, it indicates an improvement in health; other positions indicate that the Enquirer's finances are soon going to improve.

Acrobat

The Enquirer will go through periods of ups and downs.

Aeroplane

A sudden journey for the Enquirer or someone close to him. If the aeroplane is ascending, things are on the up and up; if it is descending, there will be unexpected trouble ahead. If the plane is travelling towards the Enquirer, there could be a visitor from overseas.

Alligator

Treachery, rivals, secret enemies all lying in wait.

Almond

Virginity, purity. Could be associated with the sign of Virgo.

Ambulance

Possibility of illness; if near the handle this would be someone in the home.

Anchor

A hopeful sign. Near the rim of the cup, success in career plus true love. A wish will come true soon. Halfway down, a journey which is successful. If there are dots around the anchor, this will be very lucky indeed. If at the bottom of the cup, the Enquirer will have help from friends and will overcome any difficulties. Only if the symbol is partially covered would it indicate continued troubles.

Angel

Good news. Love, happiness and peace. There could be spiritual help on the way. Any new project, especially the birth of a child, will be accompanied by good luck. If it is near the handle of the cup, the home area will be particularly happy.

Ant

Success through perseverance. This could involve other people.

Anvil

Concentration and hard work which will result in success. Also strength, stability and practicality.

Arc

Ill health – plans and projects are threatened.

Arch

A happy marriage. A fresh start and unexpected benefits. A lover proposes. Temporary states become permanent.

Apple

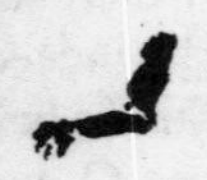

A time of achievement, happiness and success. Hopes and wishes will be fulfilled either in connection with work or relationships. At the bottom of the cup, over-indulgence or temptation.

Arm

Could be an offer on the way or a sign of protection. If the arm is holding a weapon, there are enemies about.

Army

The Enquirer will be involved in some stirring event.

Arrow

Bad news. If it points towards the handle, bad news coming to the Enquirer; if it points away, the Enquirer could be the carrier of bad news to someone else. Dots show that the trouble is financial.

Axe

Difficulties. However, also time to wield power and to clear out the dead wood. Sometimes a 'battleaxe' type of person will enter the Enquirer's life.

Baby

A baby may be born into the Enquirer's family soon, especially if the baby is near the handle. Could mean the birth of a new idea or a new project. If this is at the bottom of the cup, the indications are that a plan, or indeed even a pregnancy, could miscarry.

Bag

If closed, the Enquirer will be caught in a trap. If open, the Enquirer will manage to escape.

Bagpipe

Disappointment. I guess this could also mean that the Enquirer will be going to Scotland!

Ball

Ups and down in life but the Enquirer will be able to bounce back from problems. There could be some great stride forwards occurring soon.

Ball and chain

Commitments, obligations which are onerous if at the bottom of the cup. A knotted chain suggests entanglements; a broken chain shows that the Enquirer will soon be free of a particular burden.

Balloon

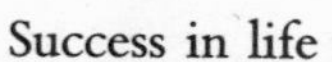

Success in life
(a) If near the rim, this will be while the Enquirer is young.
(b) If half-way up the cup, the Enquirer will be successful in middle age.
(c) If near the bottom, the success will come in old age.

Banana

Good luck and happiness soon.

Banner

Honours and fame, success in a venture. Marriage to a successful partner.

Barrel

Changing financial circumstances. A broken or empty barrel suggests financial hardship or a set-back in plans. A complete barrel shows good fortune and good times ahead.

Basin

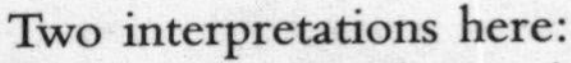

Two interpretations here:
(a) Tread water for a while, make no major moves.
(b) Warns of an illness or trouble for a woman who is close to the Enquirer.

Basket

The birth of a child, social success, happiness and good fortune in and around the home. Usually a good omen but any empty basket or one obscured by other omens could indicate domestic problems to come.
(a) If near the rim, money and luck soon.
(b) Near the handle, a baby coming.
(c) Flowers lying in the basket, happiness and fun.
(d) Dots around the basket, money coming soon.

Bat

Three interpretations here:
(a) False friends.
(b) A gift, good wishes and a long life.
(c) More than one bat, great good luck.

Bayonet

Danger, accidents, cuts, burns, etc.

Beans

Money worries.

Bear

Two interpretations here:
(a) A long journey.
(b) A reassuring person coming into the Enquirer's life.

Bed

(a) A neat bed denotes a tidy mind, rest and peace.
(b) A rumpled bed speaks of sleepless nights and worry.
(c) Any kind of bed tells of sexual activities to come.

Bee

Social and financial success plus social gatherings.
(a) Near the handle, family gatherings and celebrations in or around the home. Visitors bringing gifts and interesting news.
(b) A small business to be launched.
(c) A bee approaching the handle, a welcome guest.
(d) Away from the handle, a swarm of bees suggests business meetings, conferences, seminars, etc., all of which should have a good outcome.
(e) Money, success and honour are on the way; the Enquirer could soon be addressing an audience.
(f) A bee at the bottom of the cup means that the Enquirer will be subject to criticism or unfair allegations.

Beehive

Much activity at work, success and wealth from business.

Beetle

Money coming but also scandal.

Bell

Important news is on the way. A bell attached to a rope is definitely good news, sometimes of a wedding.

(a) Near the rim, promotion soon.
(b) Half way up, good news generally.
(c) Near the bottom, sad news.
(d) A handbell means a public announcement which will benefit the Enquirer.
(e) Two bells, great happiness and celebrations. A romance or a wedding are on the way, and any forthcoming marriage will be very successful.

Bellows

Something which has died down can be fanned into life again.

Bird

Good news, good luck coming. If the wings are extended, this is a very good omen.

(a) Birds flying mean travel, also good ideas which can be translated into money.
(b) Surrounded by a circle or a square, a bird indicates proposal.
(c) Standing birds, plans held up.
(d) Birds in a group, talks, discussions, maybe a business meeting.
(e) In a cage, obstacles, restrictions. The Enquirer may be living with a difficult person or in a restrictive situation. If the door is open, the situation will soon change.
(f) Bird holding a branch, making up after an argument, a compromise solution.

Bird's nest

Security, stability, affection and good family life.

(a) Eggs in the nest, children to come.

(b) Eggs in the nest, a nest-egg to come.
(c) Broken nest, a broken home.

Boat

(a) Protection from danger, a safe refuge to come.
(b) A journey which teaches the Enquirer something.
(c) A capsized broken boat suggests danger, unreliable people and upsetting circumstances.

Bomb

Danger. A potentially explosive situation.

Book

Various interpretations for this:
(a) If the book is closed, studies and research or a new skill to be learned.
(b) Closed book, a secret.
(c) Open book, help and success in legal matters.
(d) Open book, success in the future.
(e) Open book, an open person who does not present the Enquirer with unpleasant surprises.
(f) Marriage to a writer if a stalk is near the book.
(g) Book and pen, the Enquirer will write for a living.

Boomerang

Gossip, there may be false friends around. If the Enquirer gossips, this could come back on him. Alternatively an unprincipled course of action which has been taken in the past could also come back.

Boot

(a) Changing situations, moves are afoot. If the boot is near the handle the changes will be in home area; if away from the handle, the changes will be in the

Enquirer's public or social life.

(b) Loss of a job, getting the boot, being booted out.

A pair of boots signifies:

(c) Protection from pain or loss

(d) Business which involves local travel, sales, contacts, deliveries, etc. will be successful.

Bottle

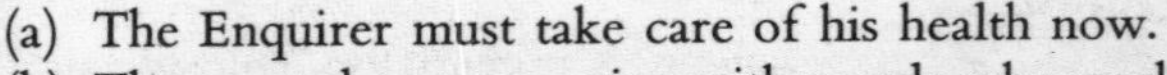

(a) The Enquirer must take care of his health now.

(b) There may be a connection with people who work with bottles soon; for instance, a chemist, publican, milkman, etc.

(c) This can also indicate parties and celebrations, or even a tendency to 'hit the bottle'.

Bouquet

Celebrations, joy, success and prosperity. Parties and social activities soon, possibly a wedding.

(a) If the Enquirer is to be married, this is a good omen for the future.

(b) All new ventures will be successful now. If there are other good omens present, the Enquirer's dreams will come true.

Bow and arrow

Bad news, spite, jealousy, rumours and slander.

Box

(a) Open, a romantic problem will sort itself out.

(b) Closed, something which has been lost will soon come to light.

Branch

New ventures will go well, time to branch out. (*See also* 'Wands' in the Tarot section on page 27.)

Bricks

Steady growth, good foundations.

Bridge

The way is now open to success.

Broom

Time to clear out old problems and make a clean sweep, a fresh start. This can be a sign of forthcoming marriage or other commitment. (This idea is left over from magical rites both of Europe and Africa).

Buckle

Defence and protection; also partnership matters will go well.

Bugle

The Enquirer will have to gather his strength for a tough project ahead. It is also time to speak up, to raise one's level of visibility, make one's point of view known.

Bull

(a) Important contact with a Taurean person.
(b) Strength and power which the Enquirer could put to good purpose.
(c) There could be arguments and bad feeling soon, the direction in which the bull is facing will show whether the anger is coming to or from the Enquirer.

Bulldog

Tenacity.

Buoy

Hope and help if the Enquirer has problems.

Bush

New friends and new opportunities.

Buttercup

Desire for wealth – look around for other signs to tell if this will actually materialize.

Butterfly

Fickle lover, a short-lived affair. If surrounded by dots, the Enquirer will waste money as well as time.

Cabbage

(a) Problems caused by jealousy.
(b) An overcautious attitude, missed opportunities.

Cactus

Courage and stoicism.

Caduceus

This is the winged staff which belongs to the Roman god, Mercury. Mercury is associated with healing, knowledge, communication, travel and magic. Therefore, these matters could become important to the Enquirer soon. (*See also* Gemini and Virgo in the astrological section on pages 25 and 26.)

Cake

Celebrations, hospitality; the Enquirer could give a party or have a family celebration soon.

Candle

(a) Help from others, also inspiration given to others.
(b) Zeal for knowledge, enlightenment.
(c) Moth near flame, a disastrous attraction (probably sexual).
(d) A guttering candle shows that someone near the Enquirer is becoming weaker in health or becoming less important to him.

Candelabrum

Sudden illumination, solution to problems.

Cannon

(a) Good luck, help from powerful friends.
(b) News from someone in the Forces.
(c) Promotion, especially if there is a star nearby.

Cap

Discretion will be needed, the Enquirer must be careful as to whom he trusts. Not a time for new or speculative ventures.

Car

Local travel, changing circumstances. This may also be a sexual symbol!

Castle

(a) A strong person or one in a position of authority who influences the Enquirer.
(b) Security and safety, good home life.
(c) A ruined castle represents ruined hopes and dreams.

Cat

If the cat is pouncing, there will be treachery, false friends. If seated, contentment and good luck.

Catapult

An unprovoked attack, a mugging, arguments and discord.

Cauldron

Sacrifices to be made.

Censer

Purification, prayer, hope and protection; also religious or other types of ritual. Patience will be needed if this is at the bottom of the cup.

Chain

(a) The Enquirer is being advised to put his energies into work.
(b) A partnership, a commitment to others.
(c) Broken chain, a disappointment.

Chair

(a) A visitor, also a time to rest.
(b) With dots around, financial improvement.

Chariot

Energy, activity, dynamic events, success in business. Matters which will need control.

Cherry

Emotional awakening, first love. This is associated with the goddess Venus.

Chessmen

Concentration will be needed.

Chestnut tree

Justice.

Chicken

Easter time could be important to the Enquirer. Pleasant new interests.

Child

May herald the birth of a child or a child coming into the life of the Enquirer. Also successful new ventures and creative enterprises.

Chimney

(a) If smoke rises straight up, things will go well.
(b) Smoke sideways, restrictions, boredom.
(c) No smoke, hidden danger.

Christmas tree

Good luck around Christmas time.

Church

Help, safety, unexpected benefits. A legacy perhaps.

Cigar

(a) New and influential friends.
(b) Broken cigar – a broken attachment or a business deal going down the drain.

Circle or ring

(a) Successful event coming, often a sign of an impending marriage.
(b) Circle with dots, a baby – three dots, a boy.
(c) Two circles, either a hasty marriage which brings regrets or two marriages.
(d) The completion of a project or the end of a phase.

Claw

Danger, enemies.

Clergyman

(a) Blessing, end of an argument.
(b) Religious ceremony to come. With a circle, a wedding.
(c) Baby or child on the way; christening.
(d) If at the bottom of the cup, a funeral.

Cliff

Danger; the Enquirer must watch what he is about to do.

Clock

(a) Improvement in health, work and money if near the rim.
(b) Bottom of the cup, a death.
(c) Time to get on with things.
(d) The Enquirer could meet someone influential and important soon.

Clouds

Trouble on the way, doubts, unsolved problems.

Clover

Doesn't matter whether three or four-leaved, good luck is on the way.

Clown

Fun on the way, but the Enquirer should be careful not to make a fool of himself.

Coach and horses

Better way of life with a rise in status. Influential friends, a more up-market home and lifestyle.

Coat

End of a partnership or friendship.

Cock

(a) New beginnings, good news, an achievement, but it may go to the Enquirer's head.
(b) Failure of plans if near the bottom of the cup. The Enquirer shouldn't be too quick to crow about himself.

Coffin

A bad omen, sad news, regret, loss. May be a forced decision to bring something to an end. Someone may go out of the Enquirer's life, but this could be a relief.

Column

(a) Promotion, success, but a warning here against arrogance.
(b) Help from friends.
(c) Broken column, failure in business, relationships or health.
(d) An unfaithful friend.

Comb

Disloyalty, deceit.

Comet

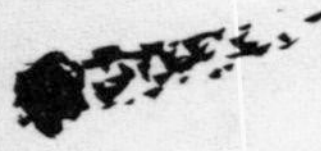

Unexpected events, unexpected visitors.

Comma

Rest and relaxation are needed.

Compass

Change of direction coming.

Cork

Celebrations, parties.

Corkscrew

The Enquirer will have to go about things in a roundabout way; he is also being warned against the deviousness of others.

Corn

Wealth, achievement, rewards, joy, fruition.

Cornucopia

The horn of plenty is a symbol of abundance, joy and fruition of plans. Good food and an easy life for a while.

Cot

A baby coming.

Cow

Relaxation, a peaceful phase.

Crab

May indicate a Cancerian person coming into the Enquirer's life. Can also show a devious enemy.

Crescent

(a) New Moon, new interest in life, success in financial affairs.
(b) Journey over water.
(c) Success for or through women.
(d) Changes coming at the time of the new Moon.
(e) A wedding.
(f) Old Moon delays, patience will be needed.
(g) Moon with star, exceptionally lucky.

Cricket bat

The Enquirer could take up a sport soon. Or he could be a good sport over something.

Crook

Symbol of protection and leadership, this may be given or received.

Cross

Troubles, suffering, worry and loss, also sacrifice. Illness around the Enquirer, sad news soon if near the rim.

Crow

Ill health, especially if at the bottom of the cup.

Crown

(a) Honours and success, efforts will be rewarded.
(b) With stars, luck out of the blue.

Cup

(*See* Tarot section on page 27.) Otherwise, success and fulfilment, especially in creative and emotional matters.

Cupid

Love.

Curtain

Secrets.

Daffodil

(a) A happy announcement.
(b) A good friend.

Dagger

(a) A jealous person will make trouble.
(b) Warning against haste, trouble on the way.

Daisy

New love affair, happiness in marriage.

Dancer

Celebrations and joy to come, a wish will be granted.

Deer

(a) Good omen for studying and taking exams.
(b) A quarrel.

Desk

A letter will bring good news.

Devil

(a) Commitment to a course of action or a person.
(b) Passion, lust, a hectic love affair.

Dice

Warning not to gamble if clouds, daggers or other bad omens are nearby, otherwise speculation should be okay.

Diver

The Enquirer may discover something soon or get to the bottom of things.

Dog

A faithful friend. If the dog is running and happy, there will be happy meetings; if sad or near the bottom of the cup, a friend will need help.

Dolphin

Safety while travelling; also help in an emergency.

Donkey

The Enquirer will have to be patient and prepared to make a few sacrifices, especially if this is near the bottom of the cup; however this is also an optimistic sign.

(a) If near the rim of the cup, good luck, even an inheritance.

(b) Otherwise peace and happiness.

Dot

A single dot increases the importance of any symbol near it, otherwise dots mean money.

Dove

Peace, love and happiness. A good omen all round but probably most lucky in the domestic arena.

Dragon

Unforeseen problems, major clashes and upheavals which will need to be dealt with rather than avoided.

Dragonfly

Good news, good events in the home, this could mean household renovations and renewals.

Drum

(a) Rows and arguments; if near the bottom of the cup there could be rumours and scandal attached to the Enquirer.

(b) A successful career involving the general public. The Enquirer could reach a position of power and influence.

Duck

Money coming, luck in speculation and any work connected with travel and foreigners.

Eagle

(a) A move of house.
(b) A time to grasp opportunities and make the most of them. The Enquirer should use his knowledge, skills and wit and make a concerted effort to reach the top. In short, he should 'go for it now'.

Ear

Interesting and unexpected news.

Earrings

Cross purposes, misunderstandings.

Easel

A good omen for anyone engaged in creative work. Dots around the easel will bring money.

Egg

A symbol of fertility and abundance. A good omen for any kind of new start or the birth of an idea or project. Can also indicate the birth of a child.

Elephant

A symbol of strength, widsom and a slow climb to success. Any venture will go well now, an excellent time to start a new business or a new relationship.

Envelope

Good news is on the way. A letter or number on the envelope may give a clue to when and who from.

Eye

(a) Take care, watch out for slippery unreliable people.
(b) Protection from problems or the overcoming of problems as a result of vigilance.
(c) Knowledge, intelligence and comprehension. A time when the Enquirer's eyes may be opened.

Face

(a) This could indicate changes for the worse.
(b) If the face looks like someone the Enquirer knows, he will be dealing with that person soon.
(c) If a face is smiling, the omen is good; if it is scowling or looks crafty, this warns of difficult people.

Falcon

The Enquirer will rise to the top of the tree and become very successful.

Fan

A warning not to talk too freely. Could also mean that a flirtation is on the way.

Feather

Instability, unpredictability, lack of concentration.

Fence

Minor setbacks in plans, hurdles to be crossed.

Fern

An unfaithful but exciting lover.

Fig tree

A lucky sign, plenty of goodies to come.

Figurehead

(a) This could refer to the president or some other kind of titular head of an organization.
(b) Sailing into calmer waters.

Fir tree

Success in artistic work.

Fire

(a) Artistic achievement.
(b) The Enquirer is being warned not to act in haste.

Fire engine/fire extinguisher

Warnings against danger and hasty actions.

Fireplace

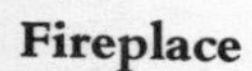

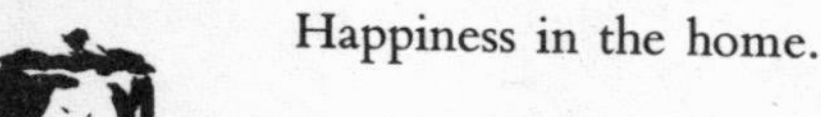

Happiness in the home.

Fish

(a) One of the very best omens. It indicates luck in anything the Enquirer is doing or wants to do.
(b) Travel or a move of house is a possibility, or just a lucky encounter with a foreigner.
(c) Two fishes which are tied together and swimming in opposite directions represent the sign of Pisces, therefore an important Piscean person may be on the scene shortly.

Flag

Some very different meanings here:
(a) Danger threatens, especially if the flag is black.
(b) Good news or good fortune (if backed up by other good omens).
(c) Death of a king or a ruler of some kind, especially if the flag is at half mast.
(d) Time to put on a good front, be courageous and go for it.

Flask

Rest and refreshment on the way.

Fly

A minor irritation; a swarm of flies, many minor annoyances.

Flower

A wish will be granted.

Foot

Good news but not immediately.

Forest

A muddle, too much concentration on details, too many people wanting something of the Enquirer.

Forget-me-not

The Enquirer either cannot forget someone or wants someone to remember him.

Fork

(a) False friends, beware of flattery.
(b) New interests if the fork is pointing upwards, old problems reappearing if it is pointing downwards.
(c) This can also point to a choice of pathways to follow.

Fork in the road

Two possible pathways forward.

Fort

The Enquirer will be in a strong position soon.

Fountain

Joy, satisfaction and happiness. There is a sexual side to this as it indicates the forces of life.

Fox

A cunning and deceitful person is or will be around the Enquirer.

Frog

A number of meanings here:
(a) A move of house or premises.
(b) Avoid self-importance, vanity.
(c) Associated with the goddess, Isis, this foretells a change in the Enquirer's life which will make all the grey days bright, bringing happiness and fruitfulness in every sphere of life. Good health, good friends, love, and protection from harm.

Fruit

Abundance, prosperity, happiness and success.

Gallows

Bad luck coming. The Enquirer's judgement may not be all that good, but neither may the judgement of those who want to hurt the Enquirer either.

Garland

(a) Achievement, honours, also happiness in relationships.

(b) At the bottom of the cup, a wreath, a funeral.

Gate

An unexpected opportunity, a chance in a lifetime.

Gauntlet

A challenge.

Geese

Invitations and social events but there may be unwelcome visitors to the Enquirer's home.

Giant

A strong person or a strong influence.

Giraffe

Thoughtlessness and tactlessness may cause trouble.

Gladioli

Victory and achievement, a bold step forward.

Glove

A challenge.

Glass

Honesty, principle, integrity.

Goat

(a) A person born under the sign of Capricorn.
(b) Enemies are around the Enquirer.

Goblet

Same as cup (*see* page 49).

Golf club

Sports may be important soon or business mixed with pleasure.

Gondola

Travel and romance.

Grapes

Various meanings here:
(a) Grapes are associated with the Roman god Bacchus or the Greek god Dionysius and therefore talk of wine and revelry; but these gods can be deceptive and dangerous so the Enquirer is warned not to allow his situation (or his wine) to go to his head.

(b) A sick person will be better soon.
(c) Pleasant romantic involvements.
(d) Visit to a hospital to see a sick friend.

Grass

A time to make oneself useful.

Grasshopper

(a) Keep on the right track as jumping around could cause problems.
(b) A friend who has been away will return.

Grave

Similar to coffin (*see* page 46).

Greyhound

Symbolic of speed, a time to forge ahead and make a success of things – in short 'go for it'. Also a good time to gamble or speculate.

Guitar

Social events which include music. Romance, even a chance of being serenaded!

Gun

Quarrels, violence, war, even death by violence. If the gun is in the home area, that is where the danger will be. Otherwise mugging and assault are a possibility. If the gun is at the bottom of the cup, there is a real danger of death by violence or as a result of war.

Ham

A time of plenty, good social life, parties and happy events in the home.

Hammer

Work to be done, not all of it pleasant but it will have to be tackled. The Enquirer may also need to be ruthless.

Hammock

Time to relax.

Hand

Many meanings here:

(a) Look and see where the hand is pointing as it may just show where a situation is likely to develop, e.g. near the handle, in the home.
(b) If the hand is open, a good friend.
(c) If the fingers are closed but the thumb showing, protection and safety.
(d) Thumbs up, go ahead now.
(e) Thumbs down, wait.
(f) A fist shows quarrels, resentment and enemies around.
(g) Clasped hands, friendship, an agreement.
(h) A clenched fist at the bottom of the cup shows that the Enquirer will have to keep his feelings and emotions under tight control.

Handmirror

Prophetic dreams, enlightenment.

Hare

Shyness and timidity. A time to be bolder. Could represent a shy friend who needs help if at the bottom of the cup.

Harp

The Enquirer will have a happy marriage. If single, a lovely romance is on the way. He will never want for money.

Hat

A man's hat is supposed to be unlucky while a woman's one is a fortunate sign. May be the sign of a visitor or of a social event which will require a hat, such as a wedding or christening. If the hat is bent or broken, plans could fall through; if at the bottom of the cup, there could be a rival enemy coming into the Enquirer's life.

Hatchet

Same as axe (*see* page 32).

Handcuffs

Problems, possibly being in a situation which is not of the Enquirer's choosing.

Hawk

Trouble caused by a jealous person.

Hawthorn

(a) Could mean problems in the home if in the handle area.
(b) Away from the handle, lucky, especially for romance.

(c) Prosperity to the Enquirer and his nearest and dearest.

Heart

(a) This has always been a symbol of love.
(b) Hearts with arrows through them, a passionate romance.
(c) Other marks with this bring extra happiness, e.g. dots – money, circle – a wedding, a heart with small leaves nearby means marriage to a wealthy partner. Two hearts close together plus small leaves, a lover's tiff.
(d) If at the bottom of the cup, there may be health problems, especially heart trouble for someone close to the Enquirer.

Heather

Good luck, promises which are kept.

Helmet

(a) This could mean that the Enquirer is going to have to fight for his rights soon.
(b) Could also mean a passionate love affair is on the way.

Hen

Happiness in the home, female visitors.

Hill

Obstacles to progress, especially if clouds are also seen.

Hoe

Hard work will be rewarded.

Holly

Good luck around Christmas time.

Honeysuckle

Love and affection which will last.

Horn

A sign of prosperity.

Horse

(a) A galloping horse means that good news is on the way.
(b) A rider on a horse brings good news from far away.
(c) A horse's head indicates a faithful lover to come. If surrounded by dots, he or she will be wealthy.
(d) Clouds around the horse's head, delays in romance, but this should be all right in the end.

Horse and cart

A move of house or business premises. If the cart is loaded, the move is good; if the cart is empty, the move could be due to a loss.

Horseshoe

Good luck, good health, money coming.

Hourglass

Decision time is here.

House

(a) If near the handle, there could be domestic strife or problems.
(b) If near the rim, a move to a better home or business premises.
(c) A change for the better. For lovers a wish will come true.
(d) On the side of the cup, a temporary move or a holiday.
(e) Cloudy, and at the bottom of the cup, care will be needed in business and personal life.

Human figures

These can throw light on the Enquirer's relationships. Take note of surrounding symbols.

Iceberg

Danger.

Indian

News from overseas.

Initials

These refer to people who influence the Enquirer's life.

Insect

Minor worries, soon to be overcome.

Iris

An interesting message.

Iron

Problems can be ironed out soon, others will co-operate.

Island

A place to retreat to, an enjoyable holiday.

Ivy leaf

Reliable friends.

Jester

(a) Parties and fun.
(b) An amusing friend.
(c) A fresh start.
(d) A warning not to make a fool of oneself.

Judge

The Enquirer will be weighing things up.

Jug

(a) Near the rim, good health.
(b) Near the bottom, extravagance causing losses.
(c) Other positions in the cup, power, prosperity and a position of importance.

Juggler

This could herald a new job or a new opportunity at work. The Enquirer will get a chance to use his skills and talents successfully. There is a warning not to be taken in by others.

Kangaroo

Things should go well in the home.

Kettle

(a) Near the handle, comfort and contentment at home.
(b) If accompanied by clouds or unpleasant omens, there will be discord in the home.
(c) Bottom of the cup, domestic problems or ill health.

Key

(a) A move of house or premises a possibility.
(b) If double or near bottom of the cup, a robbery is possible.
(c) This can indicate that a passionate affair is on the way.
(d) Crossed keys, a position of authority and honour, possibly in public life. Also success in romance.
(e) Bunch of keys indicate health, wealth and happiness in love.

Keyhole

This is sexual – it stands for the female in a relationship. Usually a lucky omen with regard to love and sex, but if at the bottom of the cup, there could be loneliness and frustration.

King

A powerful friend will help the Enquirer. A good omen, especially in regard to one's working life.

Kite

A wish will be granted. The Enquirer is being encouraged to go ahead with schemes but also to keep a realistic attitude and not to aim too high.

Knapsack

Near the rim, a fortunate journey; if near the bottom, it would be better to wait for a while before going.

Kneeling person

Unhappiness, time to pray for guidance, maybe submission to others at this time.

Knife

An unlucky sign showing quarrels and separations.

(a) Near the handle, there will be a broken home.
(b) Away from the handle, a stab in the back coming from outside one's home, possibly at work.
(c) Bottom of the cup, legal matters going wrong.
(d) A knife anywhere can foretell of surgery, injections, dental treatment.
(e) Crossed knives – violence; broken knife – impotence, helplessness.

Knight in armour

A strong personality will help the Enquirer overcome his problems. If the Enquirer is female, this could herald a new lover – let's hope this is a true knight and not just another *nightmare* in armour!

Lace

A lucky sign, things will improve soon.

Ladder

(a) Spiritual englightenment, prophetic dreams as per Jacob's ladder.
(b) Advancement, promotion, a time to take one's career a stage higher.
(c) Missing rungs, setbacks but not failure.
(d) At the bottom of the cup, financial misfortune.

Ladle

Working partnerships will go well.

Ladybird

Money worries will pass, there could be some out-of-the-blue luck to come.

Lamb

If near the handle or facing it, plenty of food and drink in the home. Otherwise, no particular shortage of necessities.

Lamp

(a) Financial success.
(b) Near the rim, a celebration soon.
(c) Near the handle, a discovery in the home.
(d) Otherwise, finding things out or finding things which have been lost.
(e) At the bottom, a celebration will be postponed.
(f) Two lamps show that the Enquirer will be married twice.

Leaf

News, good luck. A good sign for future prosperity.

Lemon

Something turns sour, others may become jealous or bear the Enquirer grudges.

Letter

News through the post, the position of the letter will show whether it is good or not. If there are dots nearby, there will be money coming.

Lighthouse

Trouble can be averted, hidden dangers will be revealed.

Lines

A good time to progress but the position of the lines and any other signs which are around them should be taken into account. Wavy lines mean uneven progress forward.

Lion

Strong and influential friends.

Lizard

The Enquirer should hesitate to believe all he is told. Treachery could be around him.

Loaf of bread

Plenty of good food and money, end of money worries.

Log

(a) Lighted, warmth and companionship. May have something to do with Christmas celebrations.
(b) Unlit, wasted opportunities.

Loom

The Enquirer will soon be able to see what has been going on behind the scenes, the pattern of events will soon emerge.

Loop

Impulsive actions causing problems.

Luggage

A journey; large luggage or lots of it may indicate emigration which will be lucky for the Enquirer.

Lute/Lyre

Success in music and the arts, also parties at home. Otherwise there could be sadness in connection with a romance.

Magnet

The Enquirer will be drawn to things which will do him good.

Man

(a) If facing towards the handle, a visitor. If the man is distinct, he will be dark haired; if not, he will be pale in colouring.
(b) With an arm stretched out, he will bring gifts.
(c) If facing away from the home, this man could be leaving.
(d) Carrying bags, a hard-working man.

Mansion

Marriage to a rich partner, a rise in status.

Map

Travel and a choice of routes open to the Enquirer.

Maple leaf

(a) Could indicate a visit to Canada or a pleasant event in the autumn.
(b) Don't waste money or opportunities now.

Mask

(a) A sign that someone is out to deceive the Enquirer.
(b) Parties and celebration.

Maypole

A sign of fertility which could mean pregnancy or a better time at work. Also an indication that the spring will bring a change for the better.

Medal

A reward.

Melon

Prosperity, a happy event, good news.

Mermaid

(a) Temptation of some kind, offers may not be all they seem to be.
(b) A seductive person who doesn't mean what he or she says.
(c) Someone around the Enquirer could be seduced or lured away.

(d) Someone who is nice to the Enquirer's face and nasty behind his back.

Meteor

Like the comet, this can indicate a sudden rise in status or a successful venture, but it will need to be worked at so that it doesn't fizzle out.

Michaelmas daisy

Reunion, also an indication that there could be a pleasant event around the end of September.

Minister

(*See* clergymen on page 44).

Mistletoe

Love at Christmas, otherwise the Enquirer's problems will soon pass.

Mirror

(*See* handmirror on page 61).

Mole

(a) An enemy could undermine the Enquirer's position.
(b) Something could soon be revealed to the Enquirer.

Monk

Religious and spiritual matters will become important to the Enquirer. A time for retreat, contemplation, inward journeys and rest.

Monkey

A flattering person who wishes to harm the Enquirer. Gossip may cause trouble.

Monkey puzzle tree

Time to get rid of objects and people which are jinxed or unlucky for the Enquirer.

Monster

Inner fears will rise up now.

Moon

(a) A love affair.
(b) If obscured by other leaves, depression and emotional muddle.
(c) If in the first quarter, new projects.
(d) If in the last quarter, the Enquirer's luck is running out.
(e) Surrounded by dots, a relationship or marriage based on money.
(f) (*See also* crescent on page 48.)

Moth

A dangerous attraction which will make the Enquirer unhappy.

Mountains

(a) Obstacles.
(b) If the peaks are clear, the Enquirer will be ambitious and also able to clear away any obstacles.
(c) With dots, hard work brings financial rewards.

Mouse

(a) Timidity could result in missed opportunities.
(b) Poverty.
(c) A theft, especially if the mouse is at the bottom of the cup.

Mouth

The Enquirer may hear something to his advantage.

Mug

Visitors, possibly a celebration.

Mule

Patience will be required, but the Enquirer shouldn't be too stubborn.

Mushroom

A real range of meanings here:
(a) Business setbacks.
(b) Expansion of one's horizons.
(c) A home in the country.
(d) Expansion and awareness and sensitivity, beginning of enlightenment, development of psychic power.
(e) Illusion, delusion, confusion; drug-induced ailments are possible.

Music

Good luck coming.

Nail

Either an injustice or a sudden minor illness.

Necklace

Love ties will be important. These are successful if the necklace is complete but there will be a break-up if the necklace is broken.

Needle

The Enquirer will be admired for his achievements.

Net

A safe ending to a period of anxiety.

Nettle

The Enquirer will overcome a tough problem by using courage.

Nun

Spiritual guidance, perhaps a good female friend to offer advice to the Enquirer.

Nurse

Illness on the way.

Oaktree

Signs of strength and courage, also of building something which will last. Health, wealth and happiness in marriage are foretold.

Oar

Help with difficulties for the Enquirer.

Octopus

Entanglement, a messy situation is on the way.

Onion

The Enquirer must be careful that a secret does not get out or that confidential information is not leaked.

Orchids

The start of a passionate affair. If the orchids are at the bottom of the cup, this will tear the Enquirer to pieces; otherwise a high-octane romance.

Organ

Religious ceremony.

Ostrich

(a) Travel.
(b) No point in burying one's head in the sand.

Owl

Gossip, scandal and allegations against the Enquirer.

Padlock

If open, a surprise; if closed, a warning.

Pail

The Enquirer will have to clear up a few things before starting anything new.

Palace

A raise in status and financial position. Marriage for money.

Palm tree

Success, honour and respect for the Enquirer and family, especially children.

Panther

Treachery and disloyalty from a trusted associate or friend.

Parachute

A lucky escape from harm.

Parcel

A surprise, possibly a gift.

Parrot

(a) A journey.
(b) Scandal and gossip – don't pass gossip on.

Parsley

Some kind of purification.

Pawnbroker's sign

Leaner times ahead.

Peacock

(a) With spread tail, buying land or premises.
(b) If clear, a good marriage; health, wealth and happiness.
(c) Success in one's career, a comfortable life.
(d) Success, fame and fortune for one's children.
(e) If at the bottom of the cup, disappointment from children, one's plans will not work out and a loss of dignity.
(f) At the bottom of the cup, illness.

Pear

A comfortable life with plenty of money.

Pen

The Enquirer will have to write some letters now.

Pendulum

(a) Changes in direction.
(b) Time spent with quiet easy-going friends. The kind of relaxed loving which banishes tension.

Penguin

Travelling south or hearing from someone who lives in the south.

Penknife

Lack of co-operation, a loosening of ties in a partnership.

Pentagon

A balance between mind and body.

Pepperpot

Arguments caused by a manipulative person.

Pestle and mortar

Medical attention for an illness.

Pheasant

(a) Promotion, present or legacy.
(b) Could be a legal loss.

Phoenix

Recovery, re-birth. This might apply to an aspect of the Enquirer himself or some kind of situation which he is in. A love affair could come back to life or a career or creative failure could be revitalized and reworked in some way.

Pickaxe

Strikes and 'trouble at mill'.

Pig

Material success at the expense of spiritual values.

Pigeon

News from abroad.

Pillar

(*See* column on page 46).

Pineapple

Wishes will turn into reality.

Pipe

(a) A problem will be solved.
(b) A man will be kind, helpful, loving maybe.

Pistol
Danger.

Pitchfork

Muddles and accidents, arguments even to the point of violence.

Plait

The Enquirer's life is wrapped up with someone else's in some way.

Plough

The start of a project which will require patience, but this will be rewarded.

Policeman

Help from those in a position of authority. If the Enquirer has not been entirely honest in his dealings, this is a warning that he may be found out. Illegal acts will definitely not work out well for the Enquirer in the future.

Poppy

The poppy has become so tied up in our collective unconscious with the waste and loss of young lives during the First World War that it still retains the symbolism of unnecessary pain and loss, especially as a result of war.

(a) Bottom of the cup, loss, sadness.
(b) Halfway up, a struggle of some kind. This could be a struggle against illness or even the need for an operation if knives etc. are found nearby.
(c) Near the rim, a recovery from loss or illness or the illness of someone else.

Postman

Important news coming, probably through the post. Near rim, swift news; near bottom, delays in communications.

Posy

Like the bouquet, this is a happy and fortunate symbol. If accompanied by other symbols of romance, this will be a new lover; if a ring or a bell is nearby, a wedding.

Profile

A new friend on the way.

Pump

A generous nature.

Purse

(a) Enough money coming in for comfort.
(b) At the bottom of the cup, expenses, losses or theft.
(c) With dots, a profitable venture.

Pyramid

This is a spiritual symbol of increased awareness. Otherwise it talks of achievements which have to be worked at.

Queen

A woman will be influential and helpful unless at the bottom of the cup where she could be meddlesome or hurtful.

Question mark

Hesitancy; caution will be required.

Quill pen

Documents will be signed.

Rabbit

(a) The Enquirer should try to overcome timidity.
(b) Amusements and fun, possibly around Easter.

Rabbit's foot

Good luck; gambles should come off.

Rainbow

Future happiness and prosperity. Look to see where the end of the rainbow falls; if in the home area, that's where the Enquirer's luck will come from, otherwise he may be luckier outside the home.

Rake

(a) The Enquirer will have to work hard and attend to details.
(b) Any outstanding business will have to be cleared up soon.
(c) Sport or hobbies should go well.
(d) Near the bottom, old grievances could be raked up.

Ram

This suggests that someone born under the sign of Aries will be important to the Enquirer.

Rat

Treachery, deceit and loss. Friends could turn out to be absolute rats. In the case of a woman, she may become involved with the type of man who could be described as a rat.

Rattle

Children will bring joy.

Raven

Bad news. If at the bottom of the cup, someone may fall ill. Otherwise, losses and sadness.

Razor

Accidents, quarrels, danger, partings.

Reptile

Deceit and treachery, malice and hurt from those whom the Enquirer thought were his or her friends.

Rider

News coming either to the home or the work area, depending upon which way the symbol is facing.

Ring

(a) Complete, a wedding or a happy and successful marriage.
(b) If near the middle of the cup, a proposal.
(c) A happy and prosperous life.

Road

Two parallel lines which look like a road show that the Enquirer's situation is about to change. If the lines are straight, the way forward will be easy, if they are wavy, there will be difficulties but the goal can still be reached. If there is a fork in the road, choices will have to be made. A bend would suggest unexpected changes in the Enquirer's life.

Robin

(a) Oddly enough, the robin is a symbol of death, therefore there could be a death around the Enquirer. In all forms of divination 'death' is often symbolic of change, the idea being that the Enquirer's circumstances are going to change radically, possibly his outlook on life will be completely changed as a result of a particular experience.

(b) Another interpretation of a robin is that there will be luck during the winter.

Rocket

Happy events to come, possibly marriage for one of the Enquirer's children. The Enquirer himself could fall in love; in this case with a considerable amount of passion.

Rocks

Unseen danger, lurking, but obstacles can also be overcome eventually.

Rolling pin

(a) A busy time in the home is forecast.
(b) Arguments and criticism from within the family.

Roof

The Enquirer will soon be married, possibly also buying a new home.

Rose

(a) A sign of great success, especially in creative enterprises; also popularity for the Enquirer.
(b) A fortunate sign for love and marriage.
(c) The name, Rose, could begin to mean something to the Enquirer.
(d) If at the bottom of the cup, there may be delays and setbacks in plans but they will still work out well.

Rosemary

Rosemary for remembrance (Hamlet). This, like the forget-me-not, means that the Enquirer is being asked not to forget someone.

Rudder

Fate is guiding the Enquirer.

Ruined buildings

Shattered hopes but also a time to pick oneself up and begin again.

Runner

Messages coming. If the accompanying symbols are fortunate, the news will be good; if the runner is obscured or at the bottom of the cup, the news will be sad.

Sack

An unexpected event which could be good or bad.

Saddle

Changes, journeys. The Enquirer should take advantage of new opportunities.

Sailor

News from over the water.

Sausages

Wining and dining. If near the handle, good times at home.

Saw

Interfering friends or neighbours will cause trouble.

Scaffold

The Enquirer must keep within the law and avoid dodgy situations now.

Scales

A lawsuit is likely. If the scales are balanced, all will be well; if they are uneven, there will be losses. Alternatively, someone could do the Enquirer an injustice.

Sceptre

Honours and rewards will come. The Enquirer will reach a position of authority.

Scissors

A separation, quarrels and misunderstandings. Look at the area of the cup to see how this affects the Enquirer.

Scorpion

A Scorpio person will be important to the Enquirer soon.

Seagull

Stormy times ahead.

See-saw

Ups and downs in fortunes but the result should work out all right.

Shark

Danger threatens.

Shell

(a) Good news, luck and money are on the way. This is fortunate for relationships too.
(b) If the Enquirer is fighting against an injustice or involved in legal matters, there will be a good outcome.
(c) A sign of rebirth, also of spiritual awareness and a change of consciousness.

Shepherd

Someone will guide, help and take care of the Enquirer.

Ship

A journey will be lucky, especially if it is connected with business. Also good news from abroad.

Shirt

A generally good sign but if the shirt is obscured, the Enquirer will lose out by speculation.

Shoe

A change for the better.

Sickle

Death or sorrow around the Enquirer.

Signpost

Look and see where this is pointing and interpret the symbols which you find there because these will be especially important for the Enquirer. This pattern may give some advice or direction to the Enquirer.

Skeleton

(a) Losses of some kind can be expected soon. These may be financial, or there may be a spell of ill health for Enquirer.
(b) Loss of a friend.
(c) A skeleton will emerge rather embarrassingly from the cupboard.

Skull and crossbones

This smacks of piracy on the high seas, therefore it warns the Enquirer to be on guard against a rip-off situation or even a potential highjack!

Snake

Hatred and enmity, plots by or against the Enquirer.

Soldier

(a) A powerful friend who will come to the aid of the Enquirer.
(b) Hostility. People ganging up on the Enquirer.

Spade

Hard work but successful results.

Sparrow

(a) If the Enquirer is short of money, this shows that the situation will soon improve.
(b) Oddly enough, this sign, like the robin can warn of death on the way. The death will be a strange one.

The usual interpretation is that an important person will be murdered by a nonentity resulting in a mystery – a typical example would be the death of President Kennedy.

Spider

Determined and persistent character who is also crafty.

Spire

Spiritual attainment; otherwise a rise in status.

Spoons

(a) The Enquirer will be helped by his or her family.
(b) One spoon, a birth; two, a proposal of marriage.

Square

Restrictions and hardships, but also protection from long-term loss or harm.

Squirrel

Save for a rainy day.

Stag

A vigorous young man. If the Enquirer is female, there will be a strong young lover on the way.

Stairs

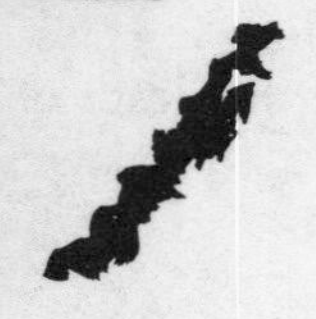

(a) A rise in status both in work and private matters.
(b) The Enquirer will experience some kind of spiritual enlightenment, possibly prophetic dreams or a glimpse of heaven.

Star

(a) Six-pointed, good fortune.
(b) A five-pointed star has magical connections which might involve the Enquirer in an increase of spiritual awareness or actual dealings with earth magic.
(c) Small stars near the handle suggest talented children.
(d) Large numbers of stars suggest problems, loss and grief for the Enquirer, but finances will be all right.
(e) A single star near the bottom of the cup is an advance warning to the Enquirer to change direction as his present situation is sliding downwards.

Sticks

These represent people. The shape and colouring of the sticks will suggest what they look like. For instance, a long dark stick would be a tall dark man, while a pale, short, fat stick would be a woman who is 'fair, fat and forty'.
(a) Crossed sticks suggest arguments and partings.
(b) Leaves clustered round the sticks mean bad news.
(c) Dots or very small leaves nearby show that the person represented by the stick will bring the Enquirer the opportunity to obtain money.
(d) A ring nearby indicates a marriage.

Stocks

An embarrassing situation.

Stork

A baby coming, especially if this is near the handle.

Strawberries

Good times ahead, possibly a proposal of marriage. Finances will improve too.

Suitcase

Travel or a visitor from over the water.

Sun

This has a variety of meanings:
(a) Happiness, success, influence and power.
(b) A child could become important to the Enquirer.
(c) A new enterprise will flourish.
(d) The summertime will be important and lucky.
(e) A Leo person will be important to the Enquirer.
(f) If this is obscured, vanity and pride will bring a fall.

Sundial

Peaceful times ahead.

Swallow

(a) This brings a change for the better in every way: in the Enquirer's love life, home, career, health, finances, everything.
(b) Near the handle, protection to home and family.
(c) An unexpected journey to a hot place which will be very pleasant. If this is a business trip it will be very successful.

Swan

A mixed bag of interpretations here:
(a) Progress and a contented life.
(b) An unexpected and unusual lover.
(c) An improvement in finances.
(d) At the bottom of the cup, death or separation from a long-term companion.

Sword

(a) This is a Tarot symbol which suggests that the Enquirer will have to take swift action in order to set something on the right path. It may indicate sudden journeys or immediate attention being given to a health matter.
(b) Otherwise this indicates quarrels and separations, divorce, loss, ill health and even a death around the Enquirer. Swords represent the end of a phase which will shortly clear the way for a new beginning.
(c) Crossed swords, strategic action will be needed.
(d) A broken sword, defeat.

Table

(a) A business conference or a family 'council' to be held.
(b) A celebration; if near the handle, this will be in the Enquirer's home.

(c) A nice new friendship.
(d) If dots are nearby, a discussion with an accountant or bank manager.

Tambourine

A time of festivities and fun.

Telegram

Sudden news; look for other omens as this could be either good or bad.

Telephone

The Enquirer will either make or receive an important call; look around to see whether this will be good or bad.

Telescope

Something which is a mystery at present will soon be made clear.

Tent

Travel. A long or short-term period of restlessness.

Thimble

A fairly fortunate sign indicating domestic changes, possibly a change of job.

Thistle

(a) A tough person who can survive anything.
(b) A time to be courageous.

Thrush

An offer will be made.

Tiger

Good luck in love and all kinds of speculation.

Toad

The Enquirer should beware of flattery.

Tongs

Restlessness and dissatisfaction, also sleepless nights.

Torch

(a) Idealism and the desire for change.
(b) At the bottom of the cup or broken; a parting, a broken love affair.

Tortoise

Helpful criticism.

Tower

If the tower is in one piece, the Enquirer is building something which will last. More often than not the tower is incomplete which means that there will be a failure in plans requiring a change in direction.

Train

A fortunate journey.

Tree

(a) Recovery from illness.
(b) An ambition or wish fulfilled.

Triangle

Unusual talent, an unexpected opportunity to be creative.

Trumpet

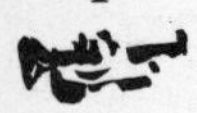

An announcement.

Trunk

A journey which has a life-changing effect.

Tunnel

The Enquirer will soon see his way clear after difficulties.

Turkey

(a) This symbol is connected with Christmas in Great Britain and Thanksgiving in the USA, therefore it means celebrations and family get-togethers.
(b) In the American theatre a 'turkey' is a flop, therefore this can mean a failure in a project. However, the turkey would have to be at the bottom of the cup for this.

Tusk

A lucky emblem with slight sexual connotations. Therefore, one can expect one's love-life to improve.

Umbrella

The Enquirer will need help and even a roof over his head; if the umbrella is open, he will get it; if closed he will not. If the umbrella is inside out, the Enquirer himself will be responsible for his difficulties.

Unicorn

A secret relationship or marriage.

Urn

(a) Wealth and happiness.
(b) Near rim, a birth.
(c) Near bottom, a death.

Van

(a) A move of house; note where the van is situated.
(b) A parcel arriving.
(c) Business travel or deliveries.

Vase

A friend will need help and advice from the Enquirer. A time to make an effort to make others happy and gain karmic rewards as a result.

Violet

(a) One violet, modesty and sweetness.
(b) Many violets, love given and received, also a happy home situation.

Violin

(a) An increase in popularity.
(b) Success may go to the Enquirer's head.

(c) Music and entertainments.
(d) An independent and very individual type of person will enter the Enquirer's life..

Volcano

(a) Passion and emotions may harm the Enquirer's career.
(b) Explosive bouts of temper will cause trouble.

Vulture

This is a really nasty omen as it indicates loss and theft, jealousy and spite.

Wagon

(a) A wedding.
(b) Breaking new ground and succeeding at it.
(c) If the wagon is empty and near the bottom of the cup, the Enquirer is better off shelving plans for the time being and keeping to familiar methods.

Walking-stick

A male visitor.

Wall

A time to build for the future but there will be obstacles to be overcome.

Wasp

(a) Problems in love relationships.
(b) Spiteful remarks. Possibly justified criticism which is painful to the Enquirer.

Waterfall

Love, joy and enough money for comfort.

Weathercock

Indecision, possibly an unreliable lover or partner.

Web

(a) Don't ignore sincere advice.
(b) Intrigue. Being caught up in a situation not of one's own choosing.

Wedding cake

A wedding in the Enquirer's circle.

Well

A wish will be granted.

Whale

(a) Success in a large project which involves many new ideas.
(b) A maternal woman who might find herself being taken advantage of.
(c) The Enquirer's mother-in-law could come to stay for a while.

Wheel

(a) Progress and changes for the better. Earned success, rewards for past efforts.
(b) Travel will be important.
(c) If at the bottom of the cup, there will be either, delays in proposed moves or impulsive action which could be harmful.

Wheelbarrow

Self-reliance and straight-forwardness will be needed.

Whip

(a) The Enquirer should not be too domineering but he will have the upper hand.
(b) The Enquirer might develop a taste for sexual deviation.

Windmill

A tricky venture which will probably work out well but it will require a lot of hard work.

Window

(a) The Enquirer will have a clear vision of his future.
(b) If the window appears to be dirty, the Enquirer will not be so positive about his aims and aspirations.
(c) Open window, new horizons. Closed window with bars, obstacles and a lack of freedom.

Wings

Messages from overseas, also messages being carried swiftly to or from the Enquirer. Look at surrounding symbols to see whether the messages bring good or bad news.

Wineglass

Celebrations, but the Enquirer should be careful not to over-indulge (especially before driving).

Wolf

(a) Jealousy from those in the Enquirer's neighbourhood. He must be careful not to be swindled.
(b) Can be a lucky sign if the Enquirer has sick or teething infants because this shows that they will soon be feeling much better.

Woman

This has to be read in combination with other symbols around. If the symbol is clear and uncluttered, there will be harmony and happy times to come. If clouded or surrounded by other bad omens, there could be trouble for a woman in the Enquirer's life or jealousy and bad behaviour coming to the Enquirer from a woman around him.

Wreath

News of a death if at the bottom of the cup, otherwise a fairly good sign (*see also* garland).

Yacht

The sign of an easier lifestyle, possibly due to retirement. The Enquirer's financial position will be much better, life will become quite pleasant.

Yew-tree

(a) This can indicate a death or the loss of a partner, also the ending of a relationship.
(b) Achievements are possible later in life; could be something special that the Enquirer has not as yet had the time to work at.
(c) With dots nearby, a legacy.

Yoke

The Enquirer should not allow himself to be dominated by others.

Zebra

(a) Overseas adventures and possibly a wandering lifestyle.
(b) The Enquirer will have an affair which will be very enjoyable so long as nobody finds out.

6

EXAMPLES OF READINGS

Jonathon

My friend Jonathon came round for a chat and a cuppa some time ago and while I put the kettle on, he told me that he was worried about his job situation. It seemed that the firm he was working for was merging with another company and he didn't know how he would be affected.

'I'm not sure whether I should look for another job or wait and see what happens at Aviation,' said Jonathon.

'Give us your cup when you've finished and we'll see what that can tell us.' A few moments later, Jonathon held out his cup and I went through the business of preparing the cup for a reading.

'There's a glove[1] here, Jon,' I handed the cup over.

'So there is.'

'Well, that means a challenge. It's as if someone is throwing down the gauntlet, and as it is opposite the handle, I don't think you know this person yet.' I tilted the cup again. 'There's a gate[2] just under the glove. It shows that an opportunity will be offered to you, this will obviously be demanding, challenging in some way. I can see what looks like a dolphin[3] near the handle. That would suggest travel, even a spell spent living abroad. You could make a home overseas for a while.'

'That's possible,' said Jonathon, 'Aviation's head office is in Baltimore. I could be sent there for a year or so.'

'How would you feel about that?' I asked.

'Oh, quite happy. After all, I've no ties, there's nothing to keep me here.'

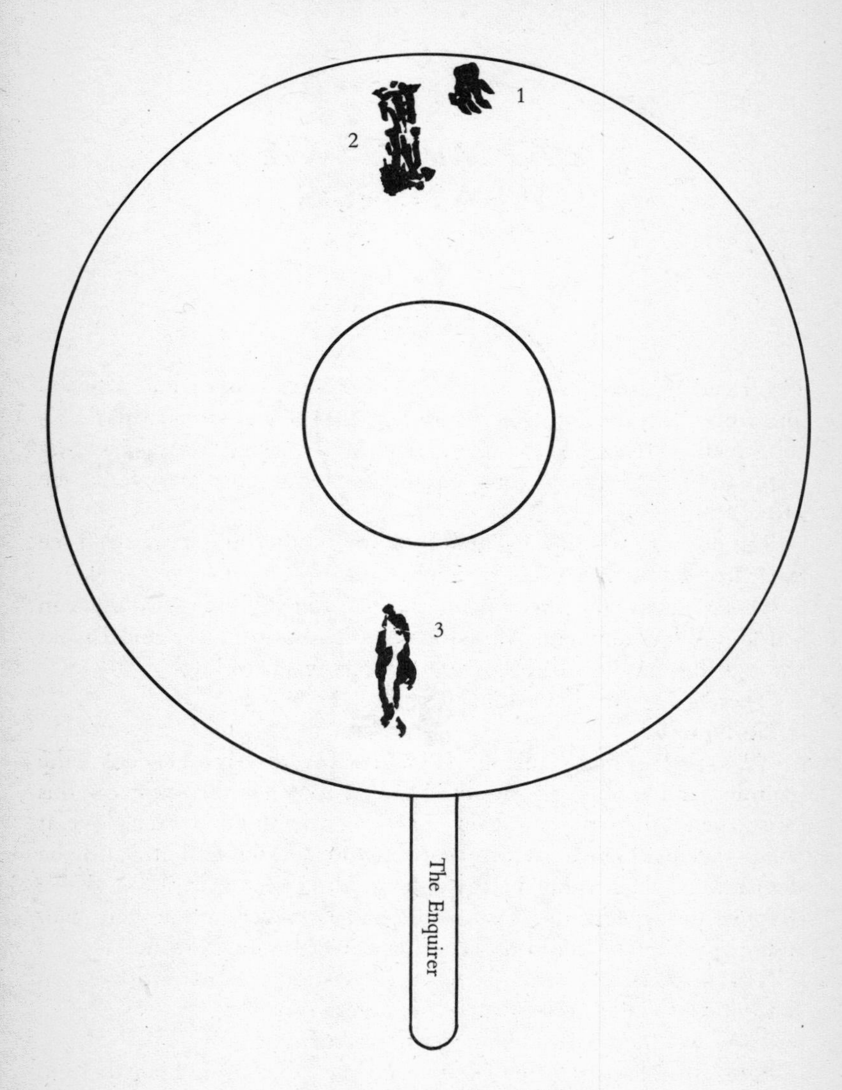

Figure 4 Jonathon's Reading

Figure 5 Penny's Reading

The last I heard of Jonathon was that he had let his flat out to a friend and had gone to the States for an indefinite period.

Penny

Penny had been to me a couple of times for readings. Her marriage had broken up and she was coping with the after-effects of a divorce on her children as well as on herself. At the time of this latest reading, she was beginning to emerge from the emotional mire and wanted to know whether there *was* life after divorce. On this occasion, we decided to try a tea-leaf reading first.

'The drops of tea which remain at the bottom of the cup[1] show tears, Penny, a sad situation.'

'Yes, I have been feeling very sad.'

I nodded. 'The Moon[2] which is over by the handle is obscured by clouds: that suggests a sense of sorrow and loss in your private life.'

'Well, that's true enough,' she replied.

'It seems that you need a period of rest or retreat, Penny, time to think and to define some kind of new future goals for yourself.'

'I've been doing that,' agreed Penny.

'The island here[3] tells me that you will have the opportunity to relax a bit more and to have a think. There is a turning-point here, it is shown by the palm tree[3] on the island.'

'When do you think that will be?'

'Judging by the position of the island and tree in the cup, I would say that something will begin to happen within the next few months.'

'Over here on the far side of the cup there is a spade accompanied by a few dots, Penny.[4] That suggests work, rather hard work I think. The dots mean money. This tells me that you will get some kind of work opportunity which you can put your heart into and at the same time earn some worthwhile money.'

'That would solve some of my immediate problems and also give me something to look forward to and enjoy.'

'I hope it works out for you, Penny.'

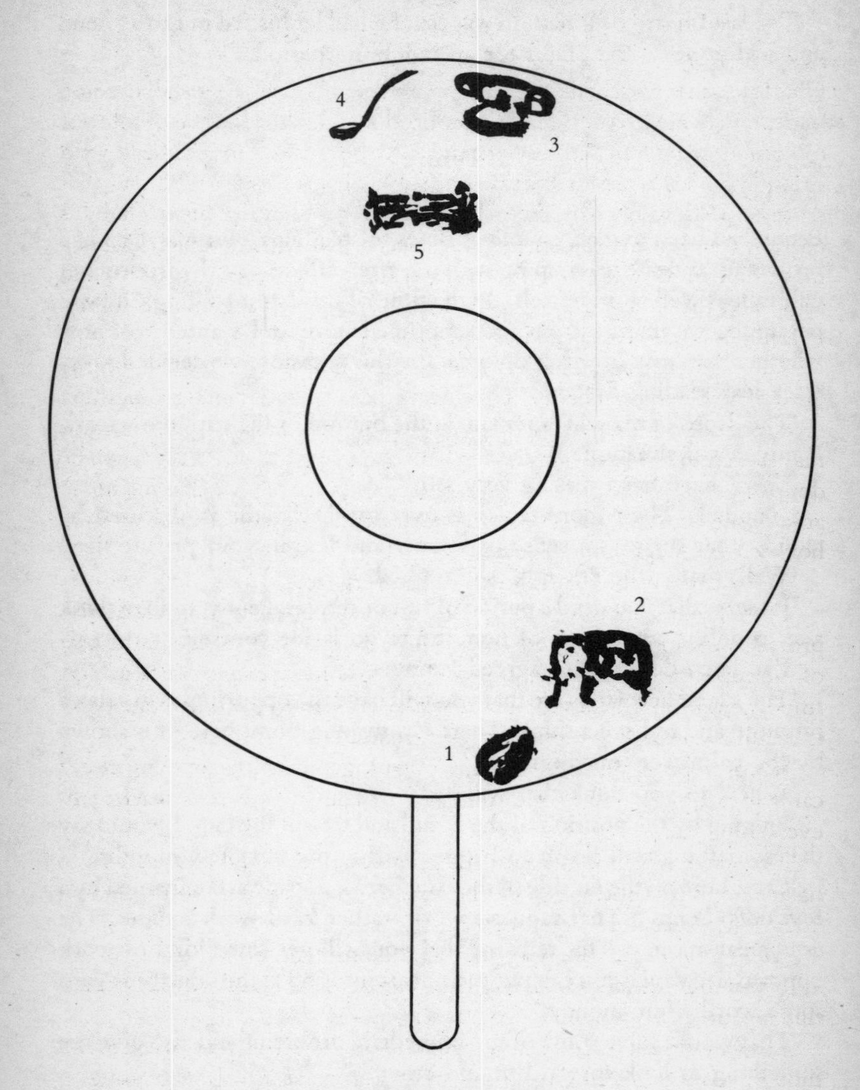

Figure 6 Charles's Reading

Charles

Charles came to see me a year or so ago because he needed some reassurance. He had designed a new product which would be of interest to computer buyers and owners and now he wanted to go ahead with some small-scale manufacturing. I read his hand to start with and that definitely showed changes in his manner of working at around his current age, leading to considerable success as an entrepreneur. I had a bit of time in hand for a chat after the reading so I made a cup of tea and suggested that I take a look at the leaves and see what they had to say. Charles was highly amused at the idea.

'This is interesting, Charles. There's an egg near the handle[1] with the head of an elephant[2] nearby. This shows that you could make something grow out of your own ideas. The egg is your own creation which may or may not come into life but the elephant shows a good deal of work to be done to get it off the ground. Both these symbols are placed in the home area of the cup, so I guess you will work on the project at home or from home at the beginning at least.'

'Yes, I'd have to, I can't afford premises yet.'

'I'll tell you something, Charles, I don't think you will work on this project on your own for very long. There's a telephone[3] here in the part of the cup which represents strangers. Telephones mean important calls. Important news from a stranger in this case. Next to the telephone there is a ladle[4] and ladles represent joint ventures.'

'It would be a great help for me to get together with someone else. I can't give up my job at the moment, of course, and it is hard to fit everything in.'

'The gate[5] which is beneath the telephone and ladle advises you to have a go at this but you won't be able to do much until you have met your future partner.'

'I don't know anyone like that at the moment.'

'If you did, the telephone would be closer to the handle. No, Charles, this person is a stranger to you at the moment.'

A few months later, Charles popped in on the off-chance to see me. 'I thought you might like to know what happened after the reading.'

'Of course I do. Did the computer business ever materialize?'

'Yes, it did. I still have my job but I can see a time coming when I could give it up. I didn't actually go into a joint venture with anyone.'

'No?'

'No. I had been chatting about the problems to a pal of mine and he said that he knew the guy who would be interested in selling my gear through his outlets. This guy phoned me and now he's shifting the goods fast. I'm looking for premises at the moment so that I can go into full-scale production.'

'That's great Charles. I'm sure it'll be successful.'

Well, I haven't heard any more since then, but I expect Charles to blow in any time and let me have a progress report on his computer products.

Of further interest . . .

Prediction Tarot Gift Set

A complete package to introduce *you* to the excitement and progressive psychic development that walk hand-in-hand with Tarot reading. A hauntingly beautiful deck of 78 full-colour Tarot cards, conceived by **Bernard Stringer** and inspirationally translated into images of beauty by **Peter Richardson**, is packaged together with a special edition of **Sasha Fenton's** best-selling FORTUNE-TELLING BY TAROT CARDS, a straightforward, down-to-earth guide to understanding and interpreting the Tarot. Aimed at the complete beginner, her explanations are at all times clear and easy to understand.

Together, the deck of masterpieces of interwoven symbolism and artistry, complemented by the comprehensive introductory primer, will enable anyone to embark upon a voyage of discovery into the world of the Tarot.

Moon Signs

Almost everyone knows their Sun sign and what it says about their basic personality. But what does our Moon sign tell us?

The position of the Moon in our birth chart affects our deepest requirements, our innermost needs. It governs our attitudes to food, our unconscious motivations, our habits and, of course, our relationships.

Complete with a simple-to-use ephemeris to find your own Moon sign, **Sasha Fenton's** book will help you to reveal the hidden power of your emotions.

Tarot in Action!

It's easy to get hold of a Tarot deck and learn the meanings of the individual cards – the hard part comes when you try to read the cards in conjunction, as they appear in a spread. **Sasha Fenton** has been an astrologer, palmist and Tarot reader for more than ten years. In this entertaining and instructive book she shares both her common sense approach and her wealth of knowledge, to produce this fascinating series of twelve fully-illustrated Tarot readings. A step-by-step guide showing how to pull together the many variable factors in any spread to achieve a cohesive and logical whole. An excellent opportunity for the apprentice reader to peek over the shoulder of a Tarot Master.

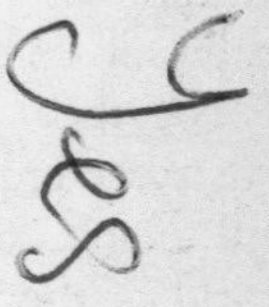